BOOKS BY ROBERT PACK

Poetry

THE IRONY OF JOY
A STRANGER'S PRIVILEGE
GUARDED BY WOMEN

Criticism

WALLACE STEVENS:
AN APPROACH TO HIS POETRY AND THOUGHT

Children's Books

THE FORGOTTEN SECRET
THEN WHAT DID YOU DO?

Translations

THE MOZART LIBRETTOS
(with Marjorie Lelash)

Anthologies

NEW POETS OF ENGLAND AND AMERICA
(with Donald Hall and Louis Simpson)

NEW POETS OF ENGLAND AND AMERICA,
Second Selection
(with Donald Hall)

MODERN RELIGIOUS POETRY
(with Tom Driver)

GUARDED by WOMEN

GUARDED

by WOMEN

Robert Pack

RANDOM HOUSE

New York

FIRST PRINTING

© *Copyright, 1963, by Robert Pack*

All rights reserved under International and Pan-American Copyright Conventions. Published in New York by Random House, Inc., and simultaneously in Toronto, Canada, by Random House of Canada, Limited.

Library of Congress Catalog Card Number: 63-7635

MANUFACTURED IN THE UNITED STATES OF AMERICA BY
THE HADDON CRAFTSMEN, INC.
SCRANTON, PENNSYLVANIA

Design by Tere LoPrete

The author wishes to thank the editors of the following magazines and anthologies in which these poems previously appeared: *Accent, Botteghe Oscure, The Borestone Mountain Best Poems of 1960, Chicago Choice, Columbia University Forum, Epoch, The Guinness Book of Poetry 1958-59, The Literary Review, New Poets of England and America, Second Selection, The Paris Review, Partisan Review, Poetry, The Quarterly Review of Literature, Saturday Review, The Sewanee Review, Stand* (England), *The Western Poet.* Six of these poems are reprinted, in revised form, from *A Stranger's Privilege.*

"Canoe Ride," "In a Field," and "Raking Leaves," appeared originally in *The New Yorker.*

The author also wishes to thank Barnard College for making possible the free hours in which some of these poems were written.

FOR PATRICIA

CONTENTS

I

In a Field	3
My House	4
Canoe Ride	6
Neanderthal	7
Harangue for Saturday	9
The Mountain	10
The Monster Who Loved the Hero	12
Parable	13
Drowning	15
Birthday	16
The Cry	17

II

Father	23
Separation	25
The Rumor	26
The Hospital	29
Adam on His Way Home	30
A Beginning	32
Today I Am Happy	33
The Doppelgänger	35

The Adulterer   36
Friendship   38
Homunculus   40
The Stairs   41

III

Descending   45
The Watchers   47
South Beach   48
The Nakedness   50
The Sculptor   51
The Two Coats   52
Grieving on a Grand Scale   54
The Election   56
The Shooting   58
The Gesture   59
Chopping Firewood   60

IV

The Boat   65
Resurrection   66
My Shadow Rides   68
The Wound   69
The Compact   71
Trauma   73
Weekday Morning   74
Toward   75
Autumn, Autumnal   76
Song for Patricia   77
Raking Leaves   78

❧ I ❧

In a Field

Here, in a field
Of devil's paintbrushes,
The circle of far trees
Tightens, and near bushes
Hump like ruins
When the moon floats loosely
Past the desolation
Owl moans wake. Here,
As if the world's
Last lovers, we
Have rung from the ruins
The whippoorwill's
Thrust of melody.
You have fallen asleep,
Breathing as the wind breathes
Among the wetted thistle,
The scented vine,
And, listening, I move
My body toward you,
When a small convulsion
Shakes your hand,
The moonlight flashes
On your teeth.
I am afraid to kiss you.
Never have I wished more
Not to die.

My House

❧

Still poised, as if in prayer,
The bleached hermit-crab,
Crusted in geologic quiet,
Has stopped going backwards. Sunlight
Falls, purified
Of memory. And you, the god
Who never was, still listen.
At odd hours, from under stones,
You called me back where slow moss
Mouthed, "rest here, rest here,"
From lace, grandmother's veil,
Or, when the starred snow wheeled,
From filaments, from window-sills.

Envy of those with a cause to die for,
Those who count their enemies,
Free to murder, free to dream
Of better things to come;
Envy of the mole, peeping
Through the snow for seeds,
Who liked not seeing what he could not see;
Of birds stuffed bright to death
With three young years sung in their throats;
Of grass, growing from skulls
Like mock hair, drying the slime of eyes,
Sealing wax chambers of turned-in ears;
Envy of monumental stone,
Secure and peaceful—envy
Because, needing something beyond
To live for, in your good name, god,

(4)

Something in me wished
To murder and to die.

It was you turned me against my father
When his tricked heart sucked like a fish
At the bland air; you cheated
My grief as the blue veins rose
On the backs of my mother's hands;
It was you when webbing wind
Gobbled at dust, spinning
In unfed corners of their house.

Now, on my boulder-strewn, green hill,
Happy in my nourished house,
A wife, two dogs, children to come,
Hating what twenty Christian
Centuries have willed,
My last cramped thoughts, sifting seaward,
Lock in my guarded hours:
Shoulders hunch to a shell;
My elbows bend to tentacles.
And there I am, dead
A silent million years, all salted clean,
With you still listening.
Hating that restless
Thought, I love it here
In my nourished house,
On my own green hill.

Canoe Ride

FOR MARK BRUNSWICK

❦

The butterfly is racked upon the lake;
I do not slow my boat to help it out.
Along the shore the quaking aspens quake.
What is this windy evening all about?

Tangled dark in dark, the evergreens
Reflect the water, which reflects them back;
The early short-eared owl knows what this means,
Who likes the way the brittle mouse-bones crack.

And with him I enjoy his appetite
And share the crooked weasel's crooked chase,
Strained sleep by day, strained wariness by night,
With crow calls coming from an empty place.

Among the ferns the nervous peepers cry;
Racoons tonight will eat the scraps I leave;
I could have saved a single butterfly,
But chose to teach my grieving how to grieve.

Is cruelty redeemed by consciousness?
Compassion is an intellectual thing.
Is sorrow sung the final happiness?
Four lonely notes white-throated sparrows sing.

Neanderthal

FOR MARCUS AND MARIAN KLEIN

❧

"The Neanderthals, 40,000 years ago . . . apparently
cared solicitously for their sick and aged. At La Chapelle
were the remains of a nearly toothless cripple who must
have been kept alive by his fellows. They not only ob-
tained food for him but must have prechewed it."
                    —*The New York Times*, December 18, 1961

Had he no God to die for, no heaven
To which his toothless, burly bones might rise,
That, so humbled, he should so hold on?

In hairy youth, had he no borders,
No hunting grounds, in whose name
Sacrifice upon the tongue was sweet?

Could that absurd, that purposeless,
That pained, vain vale of fears,
Without justice, abrupt beginning,
Abrupt into the grave, and nothing more,
Not mystery, but death—could that
Absurdity mean so much to him? Nothing
To die for, that's what makes a beast.

Mankind, your last next place, one last
Hot hate away, your gospelled eyes
Scorched into their last remorse, lips
Babbling, "Apocalypse!" to shake
The justice from the skies. Tomorrow?

My death, now that's quite something else.
I can believe in that, before sleep—

(7)

Too happy in an unhappy world, something
Grips inside, something pulls at my eyes,
Something slips in the chambers of my ears
And in the sea pours; my tongue waves
Like a handkerchief, GOODBYE, into the echo
Of the dark of 40,000 years.

Too long, too long to have been dead;
40,000 years and not yet resurrected.

Raw toothless gums, red wound,
Hold on, hold on!

Harangue for Saturday

It is a rainy afternoon.
Let it rain! Let the dismal water
Grumble in the glum gutter:
Life is disappointing, people
Are granted only the wrong wishes;
And the moronic wind, let it make its speeches
About the need for revolution
And the overthrow of all old habits.
Let it rain; there is a time for complaining.
Later, perhaps, it will turn to snow.
Perhaps the air will whiten
And, faraway, the farmer's chimney
Will turn quaint. Perhaps two crows
Will etch the only dark forms in sight,
And a cardinal will perch
In the cherry tree. Perhaps
This afternoon, someone
Will keep a promise—it may be me—
And, perhaps, by evening, when,
For an indistinguishable moment,
The snow-light brightens and one notices
The whale on the weathervane,
I will have learned to love you.

The Mountain

❦

Almost—I came so close,
As if my understanding
Might have been the trees themselves:
The mountain, with the fallen sun behind it,
Seemed across the lake no space away,
Almost like the closing of my eyes,
Near as all presences are near
By which one is reminded
Of oneself, being separated,
And, in isolation, almost understanding,
Coming so close; liquid, the loon calls,
Over the water, spilled like memories
Out of the mountainous shadow
Beneath my eyes, recalled,
But always as they drift away,
Always in their soft diminishing.

What is it you once told me,
What is it I once knew?
Always my closeness seemed to change
What waited to be understood, but seeking it,
It moved away, and the distance
That remained I understood,
At home in isolation, remembering then
I had forgotten you, forgotten
What you said, and that, too close,
You changed, dwindling away,
Even as the mountain changed,
Steaming in its underbrush decay:
Warm moss with primitive fern,

Mushrooms enchanted yellow and red,
And the dewy moth fluttering
In the splattered evergreen light;
Invisibly the mountain changed,
My closeness changing it somehow,
So that I could not see its transformation,
So that I could not see,
For I came too close, having almost been there,
Having almost understood.

Across the lake, all space away,
Beyond the pebbles' warbling
And the loons' low water sounds,
The mountain is diminishing,
It is dwindling out of sight
As the last crow flies,
And the shadow from within
Is drawing me back close to myself—
Dwindling in my own mountainous shade,
Forgetting, trying almost not to remember,
Almost welcoming the isolation,
And the dark, the dark, the dark.

The Monster Who Loved the Hero

I met a monster in a wood:
"It's not my fault!" choked through her cries,
Blowing her blue nose loud as she could,
Tears pouring from her bloodshot eyes.

Being practiced in the art,
I raised my lance to poke her through;
But I could not play out my part—
Hers was no strategy I knew.

"The ugliest need love the most,
And if you take me home with you,
You'll find, at last, someone to trust,
For Beauty never could be true."

Such fine sentiment made me pause,
Though she was not my type one bit;
It seemed against my whole life's cause
To find love and not pity it.

She saw me weaken, and she smiled.
I swear she gloated in her grin.
I must confess that got me riled:
I took my lance and did her in.

Parable

❦

Within the introspection of my dying
I reversed myself in the darkness of indecision
Because of all that hate:
The anger of birds—their shrill philosophy,
The fish uncaring and cold in their own blood,
And the animals who would not talk with me.
And I wiped the honey from my jaw with the paw
Of my hand, and I said to the quarrelsome birds: beware,
For the fox will find your nest and devour your eggs;
And I said to the meditative fish: beware,
For the carefree otter will spear you in the foam,
And to the arty beaver, the snobbish deer,
And the arrogant porcupine, I said: beware
The season when the leaves and flowers bloom dry
And the bark of the tree is acid to your tongue,
But they did not reply,
And I reversed myself in the darkness of indecision.
This was the first warning, the elemental cry,
The hate, and I started back from where I came
Where waters fountained once in happiness
And the mothering season cradled me secure,
But now the trees were clothed in funereal light,
And insects heckled me out of the grass.
This was the second warning, the change,
The strangeness; and I reversed myself
Within the introspection of my dying.
And the first warning and the second warning sounded
In my ears like leaves, like waves, like crumbling crags,
And I turned to the heedless animals and said:
It is not bad to feel you are alone,

But bad that no one's company consoles;
It is not bad to feel that you are lost,
But bad to think there is no place to go
Beyond the darkness of your indecision.
And this third warning I told the animals,
But they did not reply.
Within the darkness of my indecision,
Within the introspection of my dying,
I stopped still as I could and did not move,
And the animals came forth and licked my hands.

Drowning

Screams kicking stretched lungs out,
Biting tight cords, butting, and you
Yanked down loose with a bulge of eyes
Torn red with torn light, with ripped
Unrescued tongue, with ears locking
In lungs' packed screams, with faraway
The sick fish of a foot; yanked
From the sped sun, from rocks of knees
Drifting moonward, from crabbed, scurrying
Fingers, and you in the clenched center,
Sucked in into the scream's spasm
Of will. Past the sun's eye, far fish
Float mobile above the nursery
Of nippled sleep breathing like gills,
Easy, easy, up, up and down
Still in one place, until her kissing
Face red as bait, and your flushed rise,
Your gripped shot of spent strength
In the foamed skies of two held hours,
Fill your lungs' mouth with the scrubbed scent
Of her floating arms and her upward eyes.

Birthday

Lighthouse. Sand shadows. Burn of brandy.
A candlestick, black,
She sent with no note for his birthday.

Upside-down, the flame flares
On the dark curve of his glass.
What thought, he forgets what thought it was

That made him laugh. Nesting cries
Sharpen grey cliffs, grey weather.
Shall he return, weary buoy bell?

Surf against the shore
Bridles, neighing like horses
What his plumbed eyes tell.

The Cry

FOR GEORGE AND MARY EMMA ELLIOTT

Fallen upon my back,
I cried in the beetle's voice,
My naked legs whirring in the air,
And you—offended by my ugliness
Because you are the child—cracked
My body down beneath your foot in play,
And without the revelation that redeems,
You skipped away.

And I cried in the mouse's voice,
Whiskered nostrils puzzled by death
And curled soft feet gone still;
In the snatched rabbit's voice,
Torn muscle twitching, blood pulsing weakly,
Like regret, whitening the snow,
In that voice too I cried, shrillness
Only the dying know. And because
You are the weasel, the bob-cat and the owl,
You did the things you had to do,
And because you are the hunter too,
The useless organs were cut from me,
And without the revelation that redeems,
You merely took what you could eat.

In the infant's voice I cried—
Everything I want is everything I need!
And because you are the mother,
And milk, as from the promised land,
Flowed from your body, I trusted

When you picked me up and tricked me
Into sleep again; no other
Lie but lullaby would do
To rock that cradle in the tree.

Not by intent nor contrived by wishes,
But in pure floating because without direction,
As birds, winged like fishes,
Swam through inverted air, a depth of height
Among foaming firs, there
Were we held, mouth nursed by mouth,
Gorged free of appetite,
When, drowning up from the groin of sleep,
Choked with remembered pleasure,
Forgotten speech, the junk of dreams,
I cried out still for the needed wound
Beyond what healed love redeems,
But the bruised bell of the day gonged deep,
And you had gone for other wounds to weep.

Grown wise, humbled by the daily paper
And the responsible job,
Shamed in marriage, exhausted with friends,
Guarded by nurses haloed in sterile light,
I made resignation my reward,
For my virtue I chose humility;
And without redemption, only with God,
I gripped my breath and let no cry come from me.

With no cry on my lips,
Reminded something was forgotten,

Dreaming a cargo of appled ships,
My body's twitches frightening me,
I fell upon my back, and from my throat:
The buzz, the chirp, the whine not praying,
The snarl, the shriek, the death lament,
Sucking vowels and sexual baying,
Splashing of lips and tongue over hair or fur,
Laughter at last and speech and all songs sung—
There in my throat they were!
It was my cry, it was my voice bringing
All my voices, crying without thought
And without God, singing
Of pleasures that redeem today
To you, who, murderous and happy,
Without revelation, gladly
Go your way.

Father

I have not needed you for thirteen years.
You left my mother to me like a bride.
To take your place, I shut off all my tears,
And with your death, it was my grief that died.
How could I know that women worship pain?
My mother's eyes bring back your ghost again.

> I dreamed that digging in the humid ground
> You found, among the worms, my embryo;
> You put it on a hook—it made no sound
> Opening its mouth as you let it go
> Into the lake where, fishing from a boat,
> You watched the bulging, blood-eyed fishes float.

Failing, the strong at last learn gentleness.
When you cried out—that was your mastery!
I took a wife, but never let her guess
It was your ghost that chose my secrecy.
She needed what you would not have me show:
My need. Your strength too late let weakness grow.

> I dreamed we both rowed through a windy mist;
> The dark lake tilted where you wished to go.
> Fish scales and blood glowed at me from your wrist;
> The air I gulped only the drowning know.
> You had me hold the net, and I believed
> The fish's spastic death was what I grieved.

Screams come too easily these guarded days.
The bright, complaining, are most eloquent.

Must loss always be prelude to our praise?
Is this what mother's rising mourning meant?
For whose sake did I envy suicide?
Could death win wife and mother as one bride?

      I dreamed you threw the unhooked fish away.
      Why did I fear I had done something wrong?
      You took me home, insisting that I stay,
      But I did not feel weak, feeling you strong,
      For when you left I found the net behind,
      And angered as gored waters gagged my mind.

I have not needed you for thirteen years.
I have grown grim with my authority.
Take back my mother and release my tears,
And let a child's lost grief give strength to me!
      Dreaming, I seek your skeleton below;
      I dig the worms and find your embryo.

—Past midnight, the grass wet, his body chilled
With a wakefulness beyond fatigue.
Behind him floats a silhouette of trees,
And before, hushed, spaceless in distance,
Spread to the limits of his vision,
The horizon of the Adirondack range.
Through the pried sky, the Northern Lights,
Vibrating ghostliness, stream upward
Toward a central point, above his head,
Which of itself is darkness; a glow appears,
A green haze, a falling pause, and then
A poverty of words with which to praise
Not merely what he sees, but what he feels
He sees, a poverty of words
To praise the wordless praise itself.
—These are the thoughts he would write to her
As if the old, dark, wordless mystery
Of things was what he sought, as if
Just talking to her were not, at that hour,
All he wished.

The Rumor

PART I   THE CONVERSATION

Rumors, have you heard them: black water lying
Near tongues of bloated cattle twisted by ants,
Rumors of rotten wheat and locusts dying,
And prophets whipped, mocked by children's chants;
The only innocence they know is pain.
And echoed by the dark symposium
Of crows, filling low skies with thoughts of rain,
Heat thickens and again the rumors come,
Rumors from the governor's estate:
Plucked nails, incest, burning out of eyes;
A woman stoned to death by the West Gate
Claimed she was raped; the people moralize.
Rachel and Saul eloped last January—
She wants no sons, fearing an early death;
He finds his freedom in adultery;
They pack their lungs with lies as deep as breath.
The loves they wake to must be clandestine:
Only the forbidden is intense.
But secretly I know just what they mean,
And wish to master that same violence.
I spread these rumors as I talk to you;
I don't believe the very words I speak,
But even if I did, what could I do?
The rumors tell of rain within a week.
And have you heard, some crazy bastard hammers
In the red sun, hammers in the dark;
Muttering of doom and floods, he stammers
To his sons: they build themselves an ark.

Part II The Drowning and Last Dream

What will you do, O Lord, when I am gone?
When this green adamantine world is purged
And washed away? Let fall your final tear
In the absurdity of your concern,
And flood our mortal hill with the salt blessing
Of your unhealed divinity. For now—
Cleansed of ambition and remorse, weightless,
Without my body's fevered hope, riding
Your righteous waves beyond pain's last division
Of aspiration and repose—I know
Myself to be the breathing of your care,
The testament of your great loneliness.
And now I pity you who supervise
My death, guilty even in your just wrath,
While beyond your grieved nostalgia I escape
Into oblivion you cannot choose.
Pillowing my head, this vertigo
Of waters rocks me out of fear, and rocks
Away the vanity of worshipping
Posterity as if the dust of iron
Or the dust of bones filled more than empty space
And empty time. Now earth dissolves to sea,
Now sea to sky, and the pledged firmament
Contracts, reversed into your memory,
But, having lived, always must be: always
Your eagles glide and your kingfishers plunge
For salmon in the studded lakes; always
The congregation of the caribou
Makes holy the hour of thirst and the evening fear

(27)

While the proud beaver meditates upon
His muddy masterpiece, while Pharaoh builds,
And through the wilderness of his heart, parched
Moses tracks the Law and, dreaming, finds it
Angry in a fire. No consolation
In that conceived, strict love, cold fire, cold sea.
O Lord, will you survive in spite of me?

The Hospital

The doctor scours the child with eyes of soap.
Its corpse is covered by the sterile nurse.
Progress and hope,
Twin gods, made its death easier,
Their living worse.

For them such sorrow must be strictly borne,
Though it revives losses from the drugged past:
Her rabbit torn
By a neighbor's dog; in Buchenwald,
His father gassed.

All deaths he dwells upon become his own.
No child's nor father's death can take his place.
The bled seed sown
Blooms in the grimace still unburied
In the nurse's face.

A doll with button eyes makes her mouth pall;
At home she bears it to her belly like a knife.
When not on call,
Off hours, he dotes upon his neighbor's
Pregnant wife.

Adam on His Way Home

FOR DANIEL AND JANET NEWMAN

By the wayside, three crows sat on a cross.
It was a long journey back, the rank road
Passable only on foot, and his memories
Were little consolation. What good was past

Happiness or, for that matter, past
Suffering? Dignity, in these limp days,
Was poor payment for leaky eyes. There was nothing
To set against thin death as in the old times.

The buzzard sun flapped in his face, rattling
The stones in his wrists, his elbows, his ribs, with a tide
Of pebbles mumbling in his humbled ears,
"Nothing, nothing." Between his toes lizards

Ran where nails cracked and peeled. And this
Was not the mud of penitence, but decay.
This was the limp time, with cramped air clotted
In his nose, his tasteless tongue shrivelled dry as rope.

And then, although he was not superstitious,
It happened, as he always knew it would.
Beneath the first fruit tree, a draped figure,
Featureless, shaped as if by wind on water,

Drew him down gently, whispering, "Come to me,
I am the one!" His forked breath parted the wind,
Like clothes fallen away, and there she lay
Smiling with his eyes, his lips, and his fierce tongue,

All grown young: his forked breath breathed apart
Her foaming water-thighs, with the dark clutched
    between,
His own, his calling dark, smelling of home,
Where he leapt in the final spasm of first love.

A Beginning

Hold your rough breath!
In the waiting, in the pause,
A butterfly hovers
Motionless above a still
Untouched geranium; not one cloud
Scrapes the sky, wind attends
In the cedar's shade.
Before you speak, see,
Without an image, shadows
Are coming. You must let them come:
Clouds clutter over the hill,
Shade from the cedar sheds
On the wind, the butterfly
Alights. And here you are bruised
With new breath, in a place
You had not feared before.

❧

Today I am happy.
To whom shall I give thanks?
But you, my dear,
You seem disconsolate.
Look though, maddened
With buckling light,
Not one leaf stays in place,
And the eye follows wildly
In its own way!
No, you are sad,
And I feel no remorse;
How, without it,
Can I approach you,
Knowing that without your pain
I could not bear my own?
Still, my happiness today
Is not for you,
Though by my choosing
You are most near it.
Look how the swallow,
Drunk with flight,
In whom I lose
My restlessness,
Gathers to himself
The pronged chill of evening!

Today I am happy,
And you do not leave me.
On a red horse,
Over the spume and swell of grass,
I ride in the final safety
Of triumph.

The Doppelgänger

Down that still street where I have never passed,
No iron gateway whistles the slant winds,
No craze of moonlight crusts the steeple-glass,
No mute policeman muffles through his rounds.

My footfalls in the hall were never known,
Not known my measured, breathless, steep ascent;
The moment never came, has never gone.
There was no disappointment, no intent.

No owl was puckered for its night-long note,
No squinty bats crooked through their jagged race.
At that address there was no one to dote
On the sick moon, my sorrows in his face.

He was not there, did not curse her cringed house
Nor thin his lips, and so he never said:
I live within another consciousness;
Where I am not, I waken from the dead.

The Adulterer

Sleeping with your wife, he thought of you,
Your boyish friendliness, your boisterous talk,
How you resembled him, and how she knew
(With that unpained detachment in her walk)
When love or when vindictiveness was true,
Who was the sparrow, who the preying hawk.
And through her ease he grew to love you more,
Loved you for toughness you were tortured for.

What fascination in him did you see?
Was he that violation your fear fought,
That forced you to seek out virility?
Dreading your own violence, you were caught,
And he was trapped by her passivity.
Each one of you was sold, each was bought:
It was the heart's dear currency you used;
Through his abuse the abuser is abused.

Like children, you were fighting in a game;
The knife you drew bled pleasure from the play.
But nobody could tell who was to blame:
Whom should you kill? You put the knife away.
All you did was done in love's pure name:
The praying rabbit is the fox's prey;
The fox is banished from the rabbit's heaven;
In hell the fox is lovingly forgiven.

No appetite is clean or free from crime;
Only in our hungers are we brave.
The lion, out-debated by the lamb,

(36)

Is lowered, starved and guilty, down the grave;
Turned minister, the lamb grows fat in time,
Preaching abstinence alone can save.
But who owes what to whom, and by what laws—
The lamb's meekness or the lion's jaws?

She was not bound to him, despite her need.
You feared this more than haired flesh hungering.
She lived beyond his greed, beyond your greed.
Through her the rabbit, lamb, and sparrow sing,
And never from their song could you be freed,
Not by your violence nor by his lust's sting.
He left no son in her to take his life;
Your wounded fatherhood won back your wife.

The animals, they speak for us so well,
They populate the forests of our sleep.
What he would say to you, the lions tell;
With her he kept those secrets foxes keep.
But must the lamb define his final hell,
And must the preying hawk descend to weep?
His violation burns as your groin's fire
Blasts her with sons whose lives your deaths inspire.

Friendship

❦

Playing some childhood game, your brother
Crushed your finger in a door.
And I recall how limp your handshake was,
How your hand hid in your pocket
When you talked, as if your body
Spoke only through your tongue.

Once, walking through the zoo,
You put your arm around my shoulder,
And to show my friendship
In the jungle of my bravery,
I longed to face that tiger, pacing
His magnificent thirst back and forth
Beyond all satiation and repose.
"To love another, we kill ourselves," I said,
And you replied, "He loves best who acts
From desire and in his own behalf."

Now you have betrayed me, but both of us
Lack courage to admit it. Why can't I learn
Not everyone will love me?
Friends will ask you how I am,
And you—with your torn finger
Curled around a glass of beer—
Will reply you have not seen me for a while,
And in their hearts some door will close
That once in kindness let me in.
"You have enemies," I tell myself,
"Keep your own counsel even with your friends;
And trust to luck a woman's love

Will not unman you."

　　You felt weakened, and betrayed me.
Others have suffered such grief before,
Left behind in deserts, abandoned at sea,
The wounded—holding out veined fingers
In our most hidden sleep. Why could I not
Believe them? Tomorrow it will happen
In other places to other friends, some hurt,
Injured by the ease with which they gave,
Some hurt receiving what they sought; and I—
I close the door that let you in,
Betraying my grief which alone,
Through all the speeches of my heart,
Speaks faithfully about you.

Homunculus

The lamplight does not make their faces clear.
His breathing fills itself with sounds, with words.
He stretches toward her, whispers in her ear.
The walls are patterned red with flying birds.

Bare red birds blinking in his eyes are black.
They perch and look for me. They hesitate.
She turns, delays, but through a curl peeks back.
Her hair. His hand. They have no will to wait.

Black bone-legged birds are drinking up the light.
I know I am the one they're looking for.
Their heads thrust down, thrust up, thirst fills for
    flight.
They leave for their return. Sea. Fish. Shell. Shore.

I come to cry; I've injured them somehow.
Their breathing pleads to me, come now, come now!

The Stairs

❧

I

White, pointed shoes and ankles trimmed
By morning shade, she is stepping down
The stairs on my father's holiday
In the fuss and flutter of her dress;
And we are waiting for her, queen
Of sandwiches and admonishments.

On the walnut table by the window
Green grapes and nectarines, each
With a single eye of light, blinking
Like glass, rest by the punched cigar box—
To keep the toads and salamanders,
The praying mantis and the indian pipes,
That I will capture on this day—
As we wait for her, stepping down
The sunday stairs my father's morning.

And on this day that lasted out
The summertime my father's kingdom
Rang woods all ringaleaveo,
There by the window, pooled with sun,
By the grape-and-nectarine-lit table,
In my turtle-neck red sweater,
Stands my sister; I am supposed
To take her with me, and, knowing I will,
I tell her No, that girls get eaten
In the pine-grove by the giant's cave.

This day's goodnight—a puppet show

For which we kept ourselves awake,
By a pavilion where the lake
Smeared moonlight with the lantern-glow
White, white as her pointed shoes stepping
Down the stairs as we wait for her
This holiday morning, this long sunday
Of my father's summertime.

II

Your husband, mother, is long dead;
What will you find to do when I
No longer need your consolation?
Shall old deceptions sustain us
Though a thousand times we have exposed them?
In the knuckled shade of this twisted tree,
Peeling an orange, I watch the geese
Climb from the lake, their white throats thrust
In a misted fanfare of startled wings.

If ever I am a father, may
My children inherit this stilled hour
When the heart abandons its alarm,
Recalling at the top of the stairs
Someone I love descending to them.

Descending

FOR ISABELLE

❦

It is all falling away, the days fall faster now;
There float the first two dried and curling leaves,
Gathered by a wind into the emptiness
That only we are able to imagine,
The emptiness of ourselves and of our falling.
And having shaped the sorrows of my breath
Into the sorrow of autumnal elegy,
Why do I turn so suddenly it shakes my eyes,
Only to discover my own surprise
And the road narrowing over the hill behind me?

And have I known you in no other way
Beyond the little cruelties that turned your lip
And told me I was not a god,
Beyond the urgency whose dreams betray—
Of immemorial lovers rotting in their mutual grave,
Whom no autumnal elegy can save,
Touching bone fingertip to fingertip?
It is all falling away, the emptiness
That held us reaching, always the same,
And the touch by which we turned apart;
And now, emptied even of blame,
There is only our falling and the leaves
Curled in the wind, curling past the maple tree,
Falling and scattering like choices that we made
That quivered with revealed surprise
As the road narrowed over the hill behind me.

Conceived in the spaceless womb,

Moving through emptiness thereafter,
What can I find but terror in the laughing
Stars, knowing the trout cannot know
Of a drowning world, nor the mole,
His warm belly brushing through a hole,
Know that he desecrates a grave?
And the hawk, in his brave circling,
Will he never lift his eyes to see the sun?
And we, what more could we have done,
Before we kept in dispossession
The kisses that no mortal lips can keep
And the embrace that does not fall away
Into the passiveness of sleep?

Descending past the garden where the dead crow
Jangles on a stick; descending past
The graveyard where the bluebird prinks
In uncontemplative delight; down past the orchard
Where the cherry trees are hung with silver cups
To frighten off the bobolinks;
Down through the meadow where the summer went,
The pastoral melancholy and the scythe's lament,
Only the falling sustains me, only the falling
Seems steady now, open as it is, and near,
Almost to touch, as the consummation that I fear
No man and woman can achieve,
And perfect as the paradise whose gates—
Closing behind the hill of the road
That narrows behind me—beckon me back.

The Watchers

🌷

No longing left, she reached blurred fingers out
And plucked the shade which rattled past her head.
"What is there now," she thought, "to talk about?"
With eyes still closed, "Let there be light!" he said.

Outside, the rain-wrung willow, blossoming
Bough above minnowed bough, with orioles,
Worded her tight throat—she felt them sing,
Although the misted window drowned their calls.

She thought, "Are they the watchers or am I?"
And saw him leaning over her again:
The orioles broke, tumbling through the sky,
And all that feathered lightness took her then.

South Beach

🌷

For eight summers we had walked here,
Thinking we had lasted it out, laughing
That having called it quits a hundred times
We were now safe, that even unhappiness
Had become a bond; here once again
The gull's uplift and cry distracts me,
Rising above the cliffs and the September brush,
The brown grasshopper, the bony hare,
Goldenrod, and the treasonous ivy;
Here, without your knowing it, the sun dazes,
Everything is light even to blankness,
The blank hope of the glinting shore
And the storied sea-shell sand from which no actual
Embarkation will be made; I have returned
Here by myself, trying to think things through,
But it is vain: there is no sponsored punishment
Humbly to be endured, no judgement,
And yet—even without blame—
There is no forgiveness of oneself.

I have returned here by myself
Where, for eight years, you watched me
Act out my boyhood, with the same three friends,
Playing stoop-ball against a rock
Set in the sand, caring who won. And still
I tell myself that what was once possessed
Never can be lost, endings can not undo
The past that they define, but it is vain,
It takes death to accept death,
And my living flesh contends against

The living sun, distracting me,
Though I am here to think things through.

Two children and a poodle race along
The ocean's edge, splashing as if this beach,
The water, and a summer's day—because
They have no destination—have no end;
I lie back on my towel, cover my face
With the New York *Times*, and think things
     through
As the sand blows and, without intent,
The ocean rasps upon the shore,
Here where just last summer our dog was killed.
Under the contending sun, touched, dust to dust,
By the blown sand and the water's spray,
I tell myself that all is vanity,
Even accepting vanity is vain;
I do five extra push-ups, take a dip,
Relieved for the moment by the absence of hope,
And feel then, tightening on my lips, the fixed
White smile of the drowned.

The Nakedness: Adam and Eve

Flesh is but good, he thought, for hiding in.
    A truer nakedness he burned to see.
He took his knife and peeled away his skin,
    And hung it on the chill pine tree.

It was their minds, he guessed, betrayed their blood,
    Turning innocence to brutality,
Made her cry out in the strange heat that unwed
    Them through wedded familiarity.

Though in the flesh innocence seemed sealed,
    Each by his thought's ugliness was hurt.
No nakedness is pure when it's revealed.
    Thinking, they found their kinship to the dirt.

He scraped a snail out of its brittle shell,
    And held it in his hand—a dying heart!
What moral lay in that he could not tell
    And keep their love and honesty apart.

It is not chance that everything is chance,
    That he must join his skin upon that tree—
Whose needles rise, like nervous hair, to dance—
    Dressed naked in his lechery.

The Sculptor

The peace I feel rocks away all pain.
No father's praise nor lover's stroke brings this.
Mouths watering cannot cement a kiss;
Like leaves the stricken doe's tongue rots in rain.

Untorturing its ache I grind a cure—
The flexed doe stiffens to my mallet's aim.
In stone its cry can't curdle into blame.
I feel I am not dying any more.

That quarry mother hunted I have found:
I chisel from my heart love's monument.
Flawless her eyes where no waste waters went.
Pure, pure, her lips call from the carved ground!

The Two Coats

With mortal noises rising from the street,
She walked her curtained room and felt her touch
Give animation to the furniture:
The armchair settled in, the round lamps purred,
And on the bed, pillows took their watch.
Waiting for him, perfume of preparation
Filled the air, for whatever wish she wished,
Surely she could have it now. If this
Is love, why, what has she to do but wait,
And let the force by which her mother made
Her choice, that mother hers, winding her back
To the first act of love, just lead her on?
The noises rising sweaty from the street
Became his footsteps on the stair, and she—
In the conspiracy which she had made
Out of her waiting, her most delicate moving
Through painted scenes that might or might not come—
Pictured the coat he took from the boyish soldier
He had shot, saw, where the bullet-hole
Burned in, a golden button was now sewn.
He had promised never to wear that coat again,
And she pictured him in his Chesterfield, the collar
Shining dark as his eyes. If he wore this coat
Her choice was made, she would give herself to him,
Blessed in the ease of forces that combined,
Beyond her understanding, to make it happen.
The golden button caught the light, spilling
In the room bruised by her cry. She hit him.
He said, "I have a chest of golden buttons!"
Greedy as a king, gold glowed in his eyes

Like empire dreams, gorgeous and corrupt,
While golden light, liquid as blood, stiffened
His steep hands that bought her in the dungeon
Where she lay. Ransomed by that gold,
She bled as that young soldier bled his life
Away liquid in a field of snow, at peace,
Not to give it, but to have it taken from him;
And from the street the mortal noises wound
The golden nakedness that clothed them then.

Grieving on a Grand Scale

❧

Wailing its burst mechanical heart,
The plane plunged between two hills,
And you were dead. I day-dreamed that.
How could I mourn you if you really died?
And how, dear one, can I truly grieve
For the plain girl raped dead in Central Park,
Her mouth shaped to a cry, like a grave,
For the grubbed-nose boy by the truck,
Only bicycle wheels still spinning,
For the old man with nothing to do,
The rich man who hates spending,
For the fox, one summer dead, flies
Strumming the revealed harp of his chest,
For birds, killed by insecticides,
For the bugs? Should they be mourned too?
And for those who will die in wars to come,
How shall I mourn that abstraction? And how
Can I guard against pitying myself
When to die is to go where no hot women,
Twisted into hands and hair,
Greet one with gratifying tears?

O, not to seek out mankind in signs
And images, nor let the glutted blood,
Walking the cannibal city, go
Worshipping the strangled air;
O, not to hate because grieving fails,
Because sorrow shudders merely into art,
But to mourn softly, without hope of resurrection,
To say nothing, to think nothing,

As, through a rinsed mind, my hands rise
To take off your clothes, and faraway,
Still before dawn, the thick scent of munched pears
Follows the first wind where young deer
Do not move—their loose watery lips
Slide over their gums with a sound like weeping.

The Election

One candidate has been nominated
By both parties. He is running
Against himself. He has two platforms,
Similar, yes, but not identical.
A large vote is expected. People
Are informed, they argue their opinions;
They defend their party. Never,
They feel, has more been at stake.
The kids stop at their games, giggling,
Watching me, watching T.V.

At the University, my friends
Have decided not to vote. They
Are protesting. Historians are writing
Letters to the *Times*. Professional
Negroes, glib children of Christ's
Grace, Jews grown perfect in their
History of pain, the beatified—
All are brandishing analogies.

I, as you observe, see through this,
And have detached myself. Not
Out of principle—understand that,
Nor because I am a fatalist
And do not believe in human will,
But because I know only
What is wrong (everything human),
And can't seriously imagine civilization
Otherwise. Would you call us
Hypocrites, we whose whole virtue

Lies in our hatred of the world?
What would we do without that hate?
Ah, but our motives do not prove us wrong!

What do they see in my face that has made them
Stop playing? Go back to your games!

A trend has been established. Gestures
Of conciliation are being made.
The new president will address
The people . . . Wait—something has gone wrong
With my T.V. It is distorting.
The repairman, who seems to be talking
On several phones at once, tells me
There has been a mix-up at Central
Broadcasting, I should be patient.

The president's image is marvelously
Grotesque, his voice is garbled.
The kids are laughing wildly. A brown
Substance seems to be coming out of his mouth
And into the room. The kids are throwing it
At each other. It is filling the room.
The kids have stopped laughing.
I had not expected this. The kids
Are screaming and tearing at my eyes.

The Shooting

❦

I shot an otter because I had a gun;
The gun was loaned to me, you understand.
Perhaps I shot it merely for the fun.
Must everything have meaning and be planned?

Afterwards I suffered penitence,
And dreamed my dachshund died, convulsed in fright.
They look alike, but that's coincidence.
Within one week my dream was proven right.

At first I thought its death significant
As punishment for what I'd lightly done;
But good sense said I'd nothing to repent,
That it is natural to hunt for fun.

Was I unnatural to feel remorse?
I mourned the otter and my dog as one.
But superstition would not guide my course;
To prove that I was free I bought the gun.

I dreamed I watched my frightened brother die.
Such fancy worried me, I must admit.
But at his funeral I would not cry,
Certain that I was not to blame for it.

I gave my friend the gun because of guilt,
And feared then that my sanity was done.
On fear, he said, the myth of hell was built.
He shot an otter because he had a gun.

The Gesture

Poised to touch, the gesture
Your hand made, like light opening,
Confused the pause I waited in.
I was distracted by the sound
Of the reminding sea
Behind the sandpiper's scurry,
Fracturing the foam,
By wet leaves as, at first
Thrush-call, each one reaches,
Shivers and goes still—
Distracted by a fear that this
Was not what I had wished for,
Not what I expected.
What had these thoughts to do
With my being here, with you close
As loss? And so I missed your meaning
As you missed your own intent,
And so you remained hidden
And unknown, and this I thought
Was the last communication,
This was the human bond—
To be resigned to what you
Cannot know, to the meaning
That escapes when leaves reach
Ruffled upward from their sleep.
But your poised hand, not knowing
What its touch would give, bewildered,
Informed by its bewilderment, as foam grasped
Slap-dash at the shore, touched me
Simply, like sandpipers vanishing
Into opened light.

Chopping Firewood

🌷

Up from my belly, up from my back,
The good swinging blood floods in my arms,
Locks my elbows flat; my fingers grip
Against the grim smack of the axe
As the thud, the wood's recoil
And clap, echoes out, out
Into the quick wide weather
Of the unfailing, far-flung afternoon.

Cheeks puffed with not quite yet spent
Breath, the little nut of left air
Grows in an instant in my lungs
Into an oak, into my raised axe,
My strength's anger; it grows,
Fruited out, into my thought's words
That cry, "again, again," into
A bugle-call of first joys. Yes,
Here I am, my axe, my tree of breath,
Flames in my hair, my hands, flames
In my back and in my belly's hearth.

And there is the piled wood,
And the defied wind,
And the boulders behind the apple trees
Gone grey in the drop of the sun,
And the stopped song of the fed birds,
And the ice, the mirror of ice,
The sky in the mirror, and the afternoon
Over.

Inside,
My fireplace, my wife;
Inside, in our good bed,
The wind's grave whimpers
In my sleep.

· IV ·

The Boat

❧

I dressed my father in his little clothes,
Blue sailor suit, brass buttons on his coat.
He asked me where the running water goes.

"Down to the sea," I said; "Set it afloat!"
Beside the stream he bent and raised the sail,
Uncurled the string and launched the painted boat.

White birds, flown like flags, wrenched his eyes pale.
He leaped on the tight deck and took the wind.
I watched the ship foam lurching in the gale,

And cried, "Come back, you don't know what you'll
    find!"
He steered. The ship grew, reddening the sky.
Water throbbed backward, blind stumbling after blind.

The rusty storm diminished in his eye,
And down he looked at me. A harbor rose.
I asked, "What happens, father, when you die?"

He told where all the running water goes,
And dressed me gently in my little clothes.

Resurrection

On the taut shore, the bald skull,
Bleached, abandoned, more regular than stone,
Glistens, a little cast-away sun
Among planetary pebbles, galaxies of sand.
Dragged out again, again to drown,
By choked water, wheezing waves,
The outflung aged angel gulls
Gossip its descent; cliffs moulder,
Smoldering the anger of the drugged earth's age,
While the skull's sockets suck the foam,
Windows for eels to swim like sight away,
With the crooked teeth laughing sea-weed,
Sighing from the ribs of the deep sea-dunes.

Beyond bird-rubbed air, a skeleton,
From denial of its burned-out blood,
Rises erect in the moonlight like a soul;
Like shaped clouds clustered in, see
There is the furled skull, and there to the south,
Outstretched, float delicate finger-bones;
To the north, the cupped right palm
Catches feathers fallen from angel-wings.
Thigh-bones, knee-bones, ankle-bones, toes, dangle
Eastward, all parts are there, jointed,
All held intact, prayerful, and pure.

He rises swiftly now, rises
To the west, as if summoned, as if
Called forth and dreaming himself unencumbered
Up through space, without

A tongue, voiceless, with no lips.
The sea sparkles with the sperm
Of his rejected light.

My Shadow Rides

My shadow rides the windless air.
I listen, wrapped in animal dark,
Where silver fishes, waved in fear,
Flee barracuda and the shark,
Where, tracking through snow-stifled wood,
The single-minded wolverine
And lynx, dressed gaudily in rabbit blood,
Lick themselves clean.

Like organ pipes the booming sun
Blasts sleepy birds into the air,
And on the waves Leviathan
Can dance his oceanic care;
And deer drink honey from the dew,
And beavers build in brotherhood,
And even if this all were true,
Would it be good?

In animal dark I sing this song
To forest of eye and ocean of ear;
And what is right and what is wrong
Are not unfolded here.

The Wound

Then you were satisfied,
Having eaten me.
But the acrid rust, the peat,
Burn with the wound, and I—
Reassembling myself
In the cramped silence—
How can I tell if the odor
Comes from my own wound?

Only the wound still lives,
Sucking moist emptiness;
It draws its stringy breath,
It is my breathing,
Or, if not, if it is yours—
Who tore me into scraps:
Wires of gut dangling
Their electric chill, bottles
Of spilled fluid, crushed girders
Of bone—having devoured me,
How can your wound, if your wound
It is, still take its breath
From my shattered parts?

But if the wound is mine,
Slow odor of decay,
Wheels, detached, spinning
On their sides, leaky bags,
And there an eye among stones,
And if I am your nourishment
To death, the accuser

Cherished in your womb—
How, with my wound breathing
In your own, shall you again
Abandon me to the light,
That, in hunger, waking
Once more separate and whole,
My full share I may take
In love's fine feast?

Jack sat upon his mother's widowed bed;
Though rumpled moist from sleep, the sheets were clean.
Without consent from Jack she would not wed:
Choosing for her a choice he could not mean,
Jack walked his dog; the cool air warmed his head.
Achieved unselfishness earned him her praise;
Her gratitude taught him a lover's ways.

This marriage hid her old fidelity.
The Jill Jack loved too soon, soon found that out:
She hoped their love would someday set Jack free,
But was not sad this never came about.
When Jack's dog wet the rug it was spanked gently.
Jack organized his desk before he read,
Combed back his hair before he went to bed.

His wounded Jill, how could she ever tell
What love would do when love got in the way?
For his wife's sake this father loved Jack well;
Jack felt true gratitude, and yet one day
He cleanly shot a beaver through the skull.
Jack rocked his dog that midnight like a child,
And this one time his Jill smiled when he smiled.

When lovers love according to their wound,
There is a discord in that harmony.
Inside that room the two of them were bound.
Jill dreamed Jack's mother shook the dog angrily.
Jack dreamed a dog was dug out of the ground.

"You're one of us," was what his mother said.
And at their wedding all of them were wed.

Jill loved him in a blunt hurt child's way,
Clothing herself in pain to be a bride.
Jack's dog was run down on a summer's day:
When he cried out, his father's ghost replied,
"Who love the living must the dead betray,"
Unlocked the door. That Jack fell from there.
Dead things are dead beyond love's last repair.

Trauma

Right in front of old
Mr. Baumgarten's fruit-stand,
With a Sun-kist orange whole
In its mouth, like a grin,
I saw a white dead
Horse with a long horn
Coming from its forehead.

Two heavy happy men
Were laughing and slapping each other:
"Jake the butcher
Has done it again!"

A lady with a blotched face
Under a black shawl,
Fainted with a scream,
And another sent
Someone to call
The Department
Of Sanitation immediately,
But a man with a brief-case
Said No, call the Museum
Of Natural History.

But the two heavy happy
Men kept laughing and slapping:
"What a hell of a sense
Of humor Jake's got!"

For my sixth birthday, my parents
Bought me an erector set.

Weekday Morning

Arched, the weasel drops the unwrithed snake,
Shredded, the neat head bitten off, bones pried.
Your bed. Squared window light. Again awake!

Analyze your dream. Brush teeth. Rinse blood.
Make your tinkle, get it in the pot—
Good boy! Be serious, half your life's dead.

"Bombs," say the Russians. "Bombs," we reply. So what?
When your ass fries so will everyone's.
But your children! "Sins of the fathers . . ." No, not

Your fault tangle of arms and legs makes sons
Who cannot hide the thing you cannot show.
Hot in your eyes the bad night's blood still burns,

Looking to be spilled, to spill, when outside the window
A young cardinal flies sprung free as an arrow.

Toward

Secure in its own belly, the stone,
Having glimpsed eternity,
Watches day end, and, without desire,
Feels the first brunt of used air

Blinking the ferns, like eyelashes,
Sees, without fear, the sun's red scream
Whip stark across scuffled marshes
Where dinosaurs feed their great hearts.

Out of another silence, their heads
Jerk up and look. Some have grown old.
The humped night is whirling with spirits
Trying to decide if pain is good . . .

Autumn, Autumnal

❦

Autumn, autumnal, my heart's bell,
Staining with eyes'-shut-red the air,
Blow owls in the attic, blow leaves up the stair;
Over and over this day goes well.

Strange and dangerous is this day,
Pleasure frightens with each breath drawn,
The horse lifts his head like a hunting horn;
My heart is going and going to stay!

Song for Patricia

Blueing backward into space, blue light,
And on the shore—junk of the sea:
Lobster claws, starfish, mussel shells, anemone;
And in the forward-whitening air,
Ribbed clouds curled like a sleeping cat
Whose eye the sun blinks open to a stare
That shines upon him standing there,
Marking my appearance in my sight.
And doubting still, my eyes still see
Appearing whom I have become
Where in the sun-cat's eye I am,
Being happy, being here,
Wherever that may be,
All in the hour of the at last natural year,
With you still entering into me.

Raking Leaves

❦

Packed with woodpeckers, my head knocks,
Coaxing the drum of the tree to make its sap speak—
My sap, my boned branches, my veined leaves
Staining the wind, dizzying down
Amid a busyness of birds.

And she, in the bedroom, hands warm with work,
Smoothes out the wrinkles from the sheets
That last night's tumbled sleep may once again
Grow young, that habit, unfolded back
Into desire, may heat the purposed place
Where body's music's sung; unknown
Even to herself, as they
Who do not live by words, she sings
This place whose memories are birds,
And as she turns away, back
Into her noon of bells, in her flown eyes
Nothing like gratitude remains,
There are no debts in her farewells.

Raking, taking time quickly,
I watch my own feet move in the ragged shade
Of the shagbark hickory, burly in the blood
Of my own speed, my own strength, now smack
In the sun, barbarously bright, sight
For closed eyes, and up out again to seek,
To take, to make what I will, skill of delight
I am not author of; above, no missing God
I miss; high satisfying sky though, and below,
Chrysanthemums in garb of gaiety,

Little serious clowns, and look, beyond the brook
The fat grouse bumps across the field
And jumps for berries in the honeysuckle.

Not here, not now, one world goes down,
And, not in my head, the serious men
Chronicle its going; I cannot tell them
I am raking leaves. This day is hers,
This is my time; with us together
Two chores away, all rocking hours
Support this hour, all knocking days
Repeat this day.

About the Author

ROBERT PACK was born in New York in 1929 and educated at Dartmouth College and Columbia University. He was poetry editor for *Discovery* magazine, has taught a writer's workshop at The New School, and is now Associate in Poetry at Barnard College. In the fall of 1962 he gave the series of ten lectures in modern poetry at the Y.M.H.A. in New York City. Mr. Pack has traveled widely throughout the United States, Canada, Mexico, and Europe. He spent a year in Italy on a Fulbright Fellowship, translating Italian poetry; and has received a Grant in Literature from the National Institute of Arts and Letters. Mr. Pack has published two previous volumes of poetry, *The Irony of Joy* and *A Stranger's Privilege;* a critical study of the poetry of Wallace Stevens; two children's books; two widely read anthologies of contemporary poetry, *New Poets of England and America* (with Donald Hall and Louis Simpson); and (with Marjorie Lelash) he has translated five of Mozart's librettos. Mr. Pack lives secluded with his wife and two German shepherd dogs on a wooded hillside in Connecticut.